TEACH YOURSELF
RHYTHM
GUITAR

TEACH YOURSELF RHYTHM GUITAR

by Mark Michaels

Amsco Music Publishing Company
New York · London · Tokyo · Sydney · Cologne

edcb

Photo Credits:

Cover photo: Jeffrey Mayer/Rainbow Photography
technical photos: Barry Wetcher
pages 7, 40: Mark MacLaren
page 59: Jim Cummins
page 63: Wide World Photos

Cover design by Iris Weinstein
Series editor: Mark Michaels

International Standard Book Number: 0-8256-2201-8
Library of Congress Catalog Card Number: 77-93014

Distributed throughout the world by Music Sales Corporation:

33 West 60th Street, New York 10023
78 Newman Street, London W1
27 Clarendon Street, Artarmon, Sydney NSW
4-26-22 Jingumae, Shibuya-ku, Tokyo 150
Kölner Strasse 199, 5000 Cologne 90

Contents

Chuck Berry

Foreword

John Lennon. Keith Richard. Steve Cropper. Peter Townshend. I'm sure you have all heard these names before, and probably, you have also heard the records each has made with such groups as the *Beatles, Rolling Stones, Booker T. and the MG's* and the *Who*. What makes these players so outstanding in the rock music field (aside from their varied abilities as singers and songwriters) is that they are all excellent and widely respected rhythm guitarists.

This is a book about playing rhythm guitar. If you know how to play some chords but really want to get good at it, then this book is for you. In its simplest form, rhythm guitar is playing chords in time to the music. However, the scope of rhythm guitar goes far beyond this. Creating interesting rhythmic patterns which complement the music is what rhythm guitar means in its highest form, and that's the goal we'll be aiming for in this book.

You don't have to know how to read music in order to benefit from this book, because all of the music is written in tablature as well as standard notation. However, reading is a tool which allows you to communicate with thousands of other musicians, and I strongly suggest that you familiarize yourself with standard musical notation.

The rhythm guitarist's function in rock music is to give the music drive, cohesiveness and color. He (or she) coordinates the rhythm and chord changes of a song while working along with the bassist and drummer to create a "sound" or "feel" or "groove." He does this by having at his disposal a variety of rhythm patterns and chords which he plays in his own unique style. There is no one way to play rhythm guitar—there are many. This book covers various methods and techniques with which you should be familiar in order to play rhythm by yourself, in a band, or as a sideman or backup musician.

One factor which is so important that it bears mention here as well as many times throughout this book is *time*. You might not fully understand what "time" means now, so let's just say that keeping time means playing steadily and evenly with the rest of the musicians. If you are playing a great part but it is out of time, it won't sound the way it should and will confuse the other musicians. On the other hand, if you are playing a fairly simple rhythm but are keeping the time well, you'll be giving the music a solid foundation against which an interesting groove can be developed. Rhythm players with a good sense of time are really in demand, so remember—keep your playing steady and even.

Learning to do something well takes practice and determination. *You* must supply the determination; I will help show you how to get the most out of your practice. You might think that the only really good guitarists are the ones who play those high, screeching leads, but understand that you can't begin to play a lead unless there is a solid rhythm behind it.

Let's begin now. Remember, watch your time, and keep in mind that there is no substitute for practice!

Rudiments of Music

Standard Music Notation

Music is written on the lines and in the spaces of a five-line system called a staff.

The lines and spaces of the staff do not represent specific notes until a particular clef is added. Music written for guitar uses the treble or G-clef. It looks like this and must be written on every line of music.

When the G-clef is placed on the staff, the notes on the lines and in the spaces are fixed as follows:

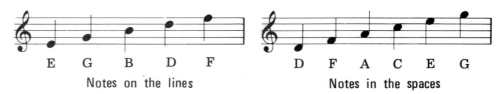

E   G   B   D   F   D   F   A   C   E   G

Notes on the lines   Notes in the spaces

When notes go above or below the staff they are written on leger lines:

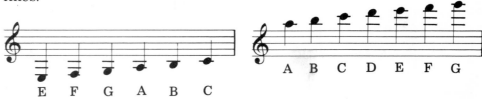

E   F   G   A   B   C   A   B   C   D   E   F   G

A whole note (an empty circle with no line coming from it) receives four beats or counts. A half-note (an empty circle with a line coming from it) receives two beats, and a quarter note (a black circle with a line) gets one beat. The quarter note may be divided into smaller fractions. This chart will help explain the relationships between the notes and how they look.

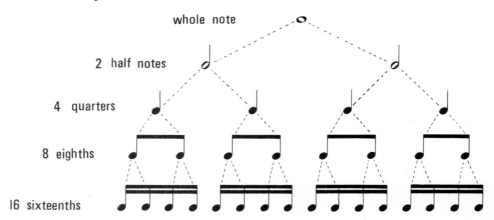

whole note

2 half notes

4 quarters

8 eighths

16 sixteenths

The notes which we have learned already are by no means the only notes possible. Obviously, every note has a neighboring note which is higher than it is, as well as one which is lower. To express this concept in musical notation we need to introduce two new ideas: the sharp (♯) and the flat (♭).

The sharp symbol preceding a note raises that note by one half step or one fret. The flat symbol lowers a note by one half step or one fret. Now we can fill in the gaps in the series of notes we have learned. In this first example, all the new notes are indicated by sharps. In the second example the new notes are indicated by flats. As you look at these examples, find each note on the guitar. Just follow the indicated string (the 6th string is the fattest; the 1st string is the thinnest).

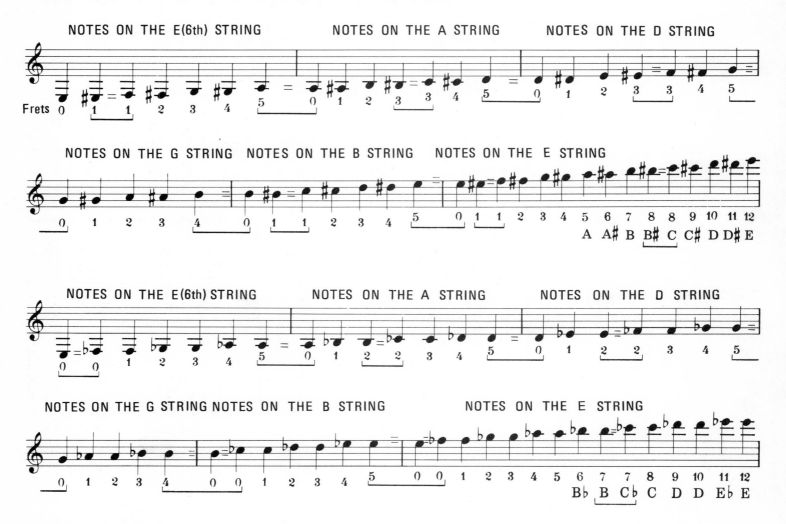

Notice that whether notated in sharps or in flats, both series of notes are the same. With the exceptions of E to F and B to C, the sharp of a lower note equals the flat of its alphabetical upper neighbor. Notes which share this relationship, for example, A♯ and B♭ or C♯ and D♭, are called *enharmonic equivalents*.

9

Tablature

As I mentioned in the Foreword, all of the music in this book will be written in tablature as well as standard notation. Tablature is a way to write music using the spatial relationships of the strings on the guitar and the notes. In tablature, there are six lines, each representing a string on the guitar. Numbers are placed in the lines corresponding to the frets on which you place your fingers. Here is an example of tablature with some sample "notes" filled in.

Whole note   Half note   Quarter note   Eighth note

Play: 5th fret, A string   7th fret, D string   8th fret, G string   10th fret, E string

A Word about $\frac{4}{4}$ Time

All of the rhythms and exercises in this book are written in $\frac{4}{4}$ or *common* time. The symbol for this is either $\frac{4}{4}$ or a " **c** " written on the staff, right after the clef (𝄞) symbol. What $\frac{4}{4}$ time means is that each bar or measure of music contains four quarter notes, each note receiving one beat. Therefore, each measure of music receives four beats. An eighth note gets one half beat. When you are counting out a measure which contains a combination of quarter and eighth notes, you should count "1 and 2 and 3 and 4 and" instead of just "1 2 3 4." This way of counting will make it easier for you to find out on which beat the written note is to be played. For example,

The first passage contains *even eighth notes*—eight eighth notes to the measure. The second contains a combination of quarter and eighth notes in the following pattern: quarter, eighth, quarter, eighth, eighth, eighth. The number of beats which each of these notes receives is: one, one-half, one, one-half, one-half, one-half. Mostly all contemporary music is written in $\frac{4}{4}$ time. That is why we will be concerned with only $\frac{4}{4}$ time in this book.

When you practice, whether or not you are using a metronome, you should tap your foot in time along with the music. Tap four beats to the measure. This may sound silly, but it will really help your time.

How To Hold the Guitar

Before continuing, study the following pictures. They will show you how to hold the guitar, how to hold the pick, how to strum the guitar and how to hold your left hand.

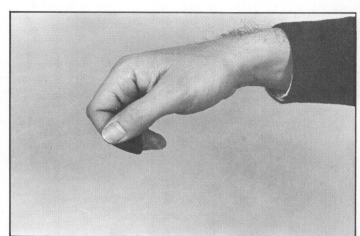

Rhythms That Are Strummed

Basic Rhythms

Let's begin by playing some simple rhythms using full chords. Use a thin or medium pick and tap your foot in time to the music—four taps per measure, along with 1 2 3 4.

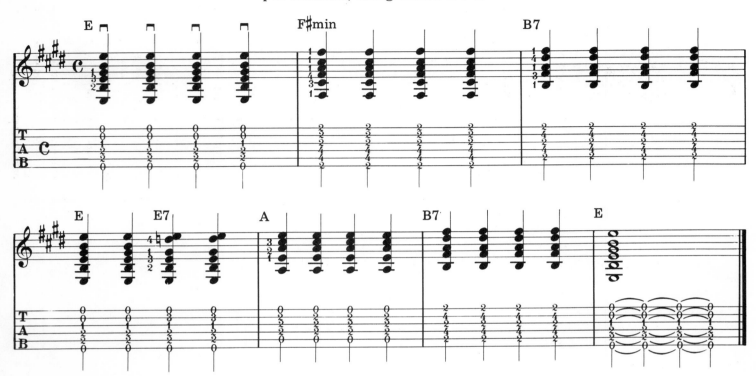

Here's the same progression in a slightly more complicated pattern. We are now using up- and downstrokes of the pick instead of just downstrokes, and there are eighth notes (count "1+2+3+4+") along with the quarter notes.

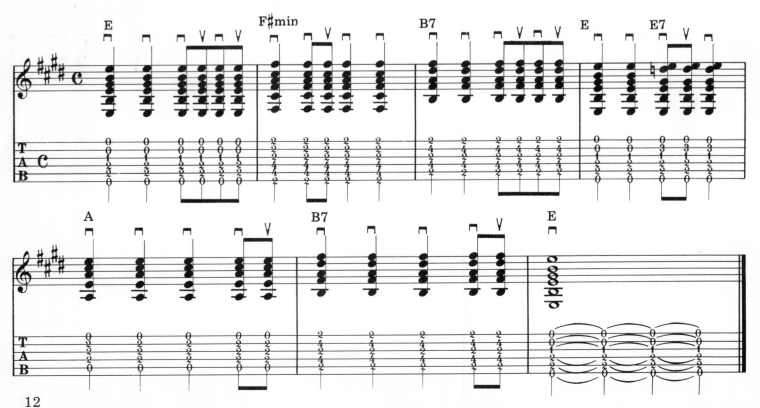

Remember not to play the low E string when you play the A and B⁷ chords. One way to accomplish this is to rest the palm of your right hand very lightly on the low E string in order to mute or damp it.

The exercise you have just practiced combines a few rhythm patterns. Try mixing them up and using your own chords to create a sound of your own. Then try this next series of chords. Try to make the chords sound as even and fluid as you can. Play slowly at first and then increase your speed.

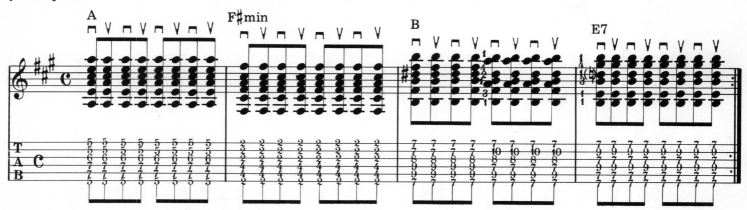

The two dots (:) at the end of the passage mean that you should go back to the beginning and repeat the whole thing. The next few rhythms introduce *rests*. When a rest appears in the music, you are to not play for the duration of the rest (thus the name "rest"). That is, if you see a quarter rest (♩) you are to rest for one beat—count one beat before going on to the next chord or note. If you see an eighth rest (♪), count one half beat without playing anything before you go on. This is the pattern for the next rhythm:

1	**+**	**2**	**+**	**3**	**+**	**4**	**+**
play		rest		play		rest	

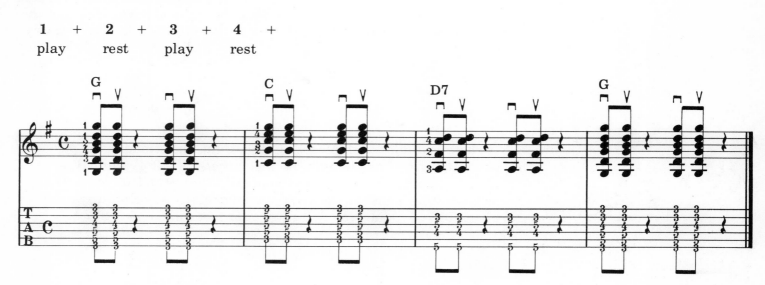

When playing the D⁷ chord, you can mute the high E string by touching it lightly with the third (ring) finger of your right hand. Or, you can just not play the string at all, but this may take a little more control in your right-hand strumming technique than you may have at this point.

Here are some more rhythms using eighth-note patterns and rests. You should try practicing with a metronome and gradually increase your speed as you hear your playing becoming more fluid.

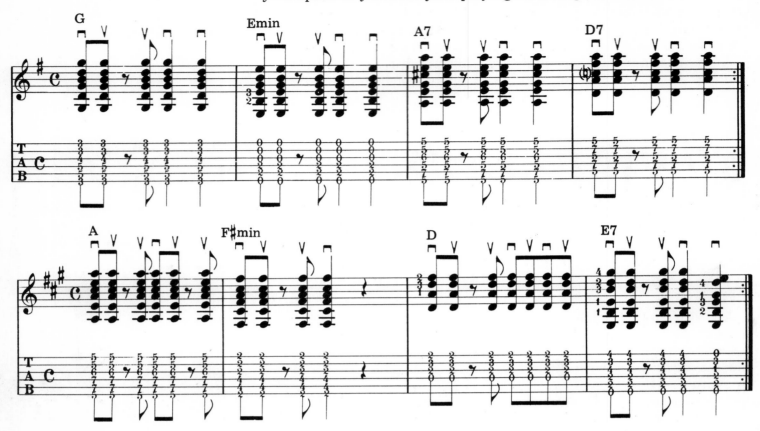

You may have realized by now that the up- and downstrokes of the pick always correspond to the rhythm of the music in the following way:

count	**1**	**+**	**2**	**+**	**3**	**+**	**4**	**+**
pick	down	up	down	up	down	up	down	up

There is a relationship between the count, the stroke of the pick and the tapping of your foot. On the *downbeats* (1 2 3 4) you will always pick or strum down (⊓) and you will bring your foot down. On the *upbeats* (the "ands" in between the numbers) you will always pick or strum up (V) and you will raise your foot up.

Power Chords

Now you have a few basic rhythms down. We can begin to work with them in order to make your playing sound more like what you might hear on a record. Rock rhythm guitarists often play simple chords in a very aggressive way to get a really chunky, "fat" sound. Think of the rhythms you hear on some *Rolling Stones* records, like "Satisfaction" or "Tumbling Dice." The characteristics of this kind of playing are:

1. Attack
2. Sustain
3. Tone

Let's look at *attack*. If you hit the strings hard when playing (the symbol for this in musical notation is a $>$ placed above the chord or note), the strings will vibrate longer and will *sustain* the sound longer than if you hit them less forcefully. This is true if you are playing on an acoustic as well as an electric instrument. Try the following rhythms using this concept. Strike all of the strings at once with one downward movement of the pick (we will temporarily deal with only downstrokes now, as it is more difficult to get a "hard" sound with upstrokes).

Play between the two pickups on an electric and right over the sound-hole if you are using an acoustic.

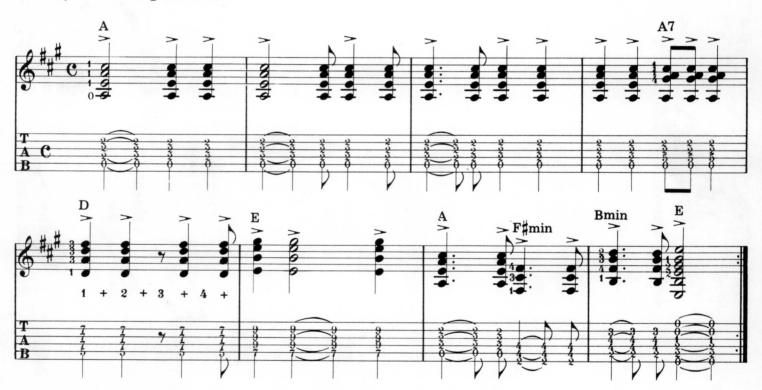

For some chords (like the F# minor and B minor) you are only playing three or four notes instead of full chords. These are known as *partial chords* and we will deal with them in detail a little later on.

The third characteristic of rock power chords is *tone*. If you have an acoustic, then there isn't much you can do to vary your tone except strike the strings closer to either the bridge or the fingerboard. Experiment. You will find that if you play nearer to the bridge, you will get a crisp, thin sound and if you play nearer the fingerboard you will get a fuller, more bassy sound. It's this "fat" sound that you should aim for.

On an electric, I would suggest adjusting your controls in the following way in order to get a powerful rhythm sound. Use the middle pickup position, which should activate both pickups (except on most Fender Stratocasters). Cut back slightly on your high end (turn down the treble on both pickups) and keep your volume all the way up. On your amp, set the volume on about 5, or wherever the sound starts to distort (sound fuzzy). Put your Bass on 3, Midrange on about 6 and Treble on about 8. Keep your Bright switch "Off" if your amp has one. If your amp has a Master Volume control, turn the amp (channel) volume all the way up to 10 and play with the Master Volume to see where it gives you the best distortion without being outrageously loud.

IMPORTANT! Any amp will distort if you turn all of the controls all the way up, but you will probably also blow it up, so *be careful*! Treat your amp gently and sensibly and it will work for you.

Try the following rhythms.

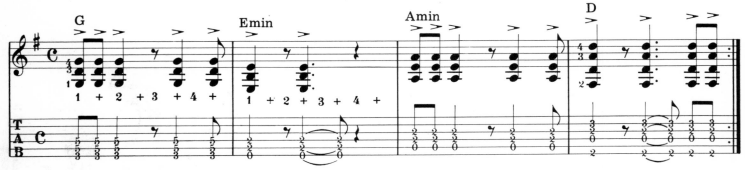

On the D chord you've just learned, mute the A string with your second finger.

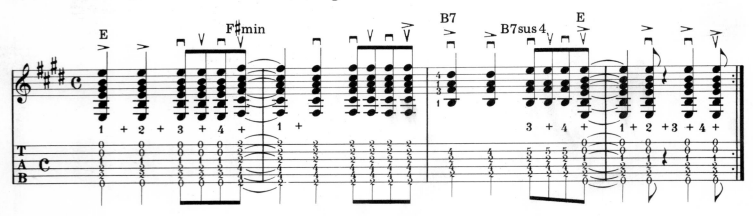

You should now work on trying to get an even chord sound while keeping the time steady. We are back to using up- and downstrokes, although for some rhythms, just downstrokes sound better. Experiment with both kinds of strumming and try to make your up- and downstrokes sound equal in terms of *attack, sustain* and *tone*. It is natural for the downstrokes to accentuate the bass strings and the upstrokes to accentuate the high strings so you must try to correct for this by striking all of the strings at once, evenly, so that all of the notes in the chord will sound at equal volume.

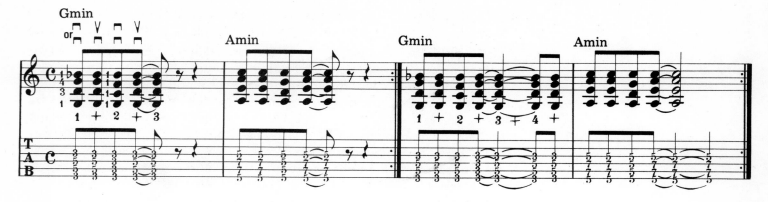

Listen to how this chordal riff sounds different when you use only downstrokes compared with when you use up- and downstrokes. In this next one, *slide* from the G minor to the A minor. When you slide, you won't have to strum again because the strings will still be vibrating. That is, the notes will sustain if you attack them vigorously; therefore the A minor chord will sustain based on the vibrations from the G minor.

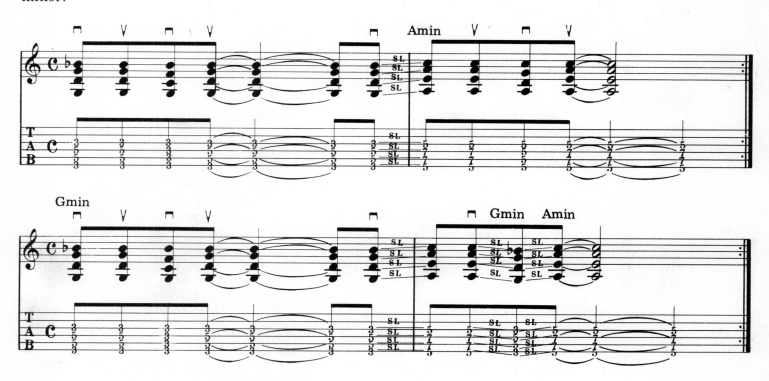

By studying the four examples above, you can see that we have developed an interesting rhythm. It's not magic—it just takes practice and familiarity with your instrument. Already you know quite a few rhythm patterns, strumming styles and chord changes, so try to create unique rhythms by experimenting. But first, read the next section in order to better understand how various rhythm patterns can be developed.

Chord Relationships

You might be wondering why some chords sound right in progressions and some don't. For example, if you start out a rhythm with a C Major chord, then go to an A minor and then an F♯ Major, the F♯ will sound "off" or wrong. The reason for this is that for every key you play in, there are certain chords which belong to that key in a musical sense and some that don't. An F♯ chord does not naturally occur in the key of C Major, going back to the example above. Here is a short list of keys and chords. Try them out in combinations. Make up your own progressions and see which ones sound good and which don't. Later on I will give you specific examples of some common rock progressions.

Key	Chords
A	D, E(7), F♯ min(7), C♯ min(7), Bmin(7)
C	F, G(7), Dmin(7), Emin(7), Amin(7)
D	G, A(7), Emin(7), F♯ min(7), Bmin(7)
E	A, B(7), F♯ min(7), G♯ min(7), C♯ min(7)
F	B ,C(7), Gmin(7), Amin(7), Dmin(7)
G	C, D(7), Amin(7), Bmin(7), Emin(7)
Amin	Dmin., E(7), G(7), C, F
Dmin	Gmin., A(7), C(7), F, B♭
Emin	Amin., B(7), D(7), G, C

Partial Chords

You do not have to play all six strings to play good rock rhythm guitar. Actually, it is not really desirable to have a rhythm guitarist who plays that way. Besides laying down the chords in time, an important function of rhythm guitar is accentuating the music in various ways. This can best be accomplished by playing partial chords, because you have a greater choice of notes than when you are playing five or six string (full) chords. By the end of this chapter you will fully understand what I have just said.

Now, here are some rhythms using partial chords. In the first measure of each the full chords will be played. Then, in the following measures, you will see how each full chord can be broken down and how using partial chords gives you a far more interesting sound than does strumming across all six strings.

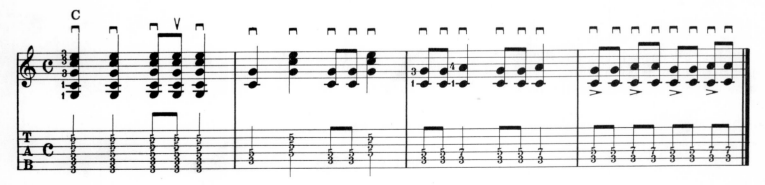

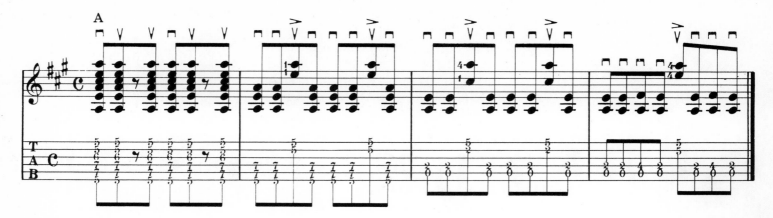

In the first example above (the rhythm in C Major), we are breaking down the C Major chord and playing the notes that make it up, C, E and G in various combinations. You can play the notes C-E-G, C-G-E, G-E-C, G-C-E, E-C-G or E-G-C and no matter which combination you play, the resulting chord will be a C Major. Also, you can sometimes play just two of the notes in a chord (as in the second measure, where you are playing just C and G). A chord which contains the right notes (like G-C-E) but which doesn't start on the note which gives the chord its name (like C̲-G-E) is called an *inversion* of that chord.

Now look back at the second example (the rhythm using an A Major chord). In the second and third measures, we are accenting the second and fourth beats. In most rock music, the accent falls on the second and fourth beats. That's where the drummer usually hits his snare drum, and if the rhythm guitarist also accents these beats, the music will have an extra "sock" to it.

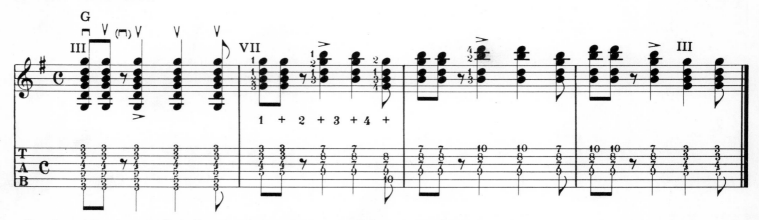

In the above example (the G Major rhythm), the accent is on the upbeat—the "and" in between the second and third beats. This kind of accent is characteristic of music like Jamaican *reggae*. But generally, in modern rock music, the second and fourth beats of each measure are accented.

The Roman numeral above the staff is a symbol for the position in which you are supposed to play. This means that if you see a III above the staff, you should move your left hand up to the third fret so that you first finger can play the notes on that fret, your second finger can play the notes on the fourth fret, your third finger can cover the fifth fret and your fourth finger can play the notes on the sixth fret. Similarly, for the seventh (VII) position, your four fingers will, in order, cover the notes on the seventh, eighth, ninth and tenth frets. Playing "in position" is very important because it allows you to cover many notes, from high to low, without jumping around all over the fingerboard. Roman numerals will be used to tell you which position to play in throughout the rest of the book.

If you look carefully at what you're playing in the preceding rhythm, you will notice that all you are really doing is playing a G Major chord in different inversions and positions. Yet you can hear quite a difference in sound between the rhythm in measure one and the rhythm in measure four. Here are some common rock progressions using various inversions of basic chords played in position.

The first two examples use basically the same progression: D, Bmin, G, A^7. In the second rhythm we are substituting an Emin(^{7}) for the G chord. The third progression goes D, C, G, D. This has been used a lot in rock tunes, such as in "Takin' Care of Business" by *Bachman-Turner Overdrive*. The last progression is also very common and can be heard in a similar form on B. W. Stevenson's hit "My Maria." Later on I will go into some more basic music theory so that you will understand how various progressions come about and how and when you can substitute certain chords for others within chord progressions.

Peter Townshend

Rhythms That Are Picked

Alternating Bass

Up until now we have been dealing with strumming the guitar to produce a rhythm pattern. It is also important to know how to pick notes in order to create a rhythm. The first kind of rhythm we will work on combines strumming *and* picking and is called the *alternating bass rhythm*. It's called this because in its simplest form, you first play a bass note, then a chord, then a bass note, then a chord and keep repeating this bass note-chord-bass note pattern.

The alternating bass rhythm comes from blues-folk and country music but is used much in rock music. It can be heard on many hit records, such as Rod Stewart's "Maggie Mae," *Wings'* "Band on the Run" and Peter Frampton's "Show Me The Way." Here are some basic rhythm patterns using the alternating bass. Remember, play them slowly at first and then increase your speed.

22

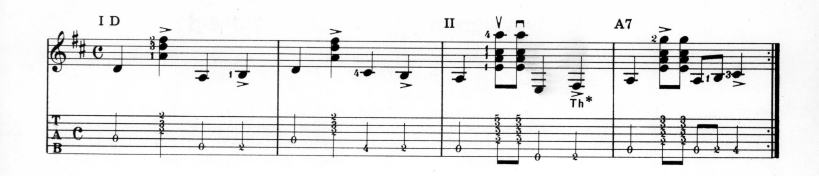

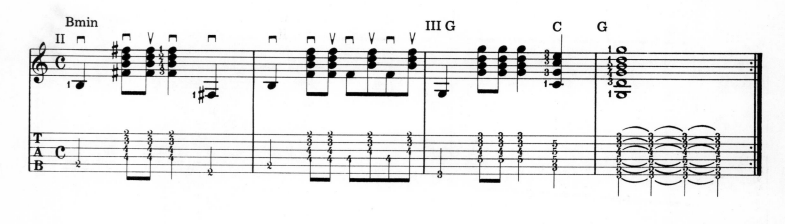

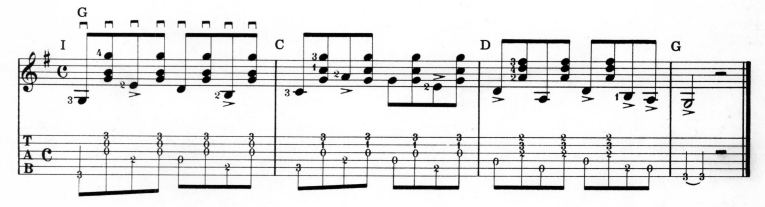

*The "Th" is an abbreviation for Thumb and refers to the thumb on your left hand.
You should use your thumb whenever convenient to play notes on the two low strings.
It *is* a finger, so why not use it?

Arpeggios

We will now cover a rhythm style in which you only pick the notes, as opposed to the alternating bass in which you picked and strummed and the power chords, which you strummed. If you take the notes which make up a chord and pick them out in a certain pattern, you will be playing an *arpeggio*. The rhythm that comes from this technique is known as an arpeggiated rhythm. Usually, you will start by playing the low (bass) notes first, then go up to the high notes and then work your way back down to the low notes. Here is an example of an arpeggio over a G Major bar chord played in the third (III) position.

There are two ways of playing an arpeggio. One, you can leave your fingers down throughout the whole thing as if you were getting ready to strum the full chord. This technique has the effect of letting the notes ring out (sustain) in an overlapping kind of way. At the end of an arpeggio played this way, you can actually hear the chord (even though you haven't strummed it!), since the notes which make it up have been played in order and are still sounding.

The second technique for playing an arpeggio is to pick up your finger after playing each note. Since a note won't sound after you take your finger off the string, this way of playing gives you a choppier sound than the first arpeggio technique does.

Here is another example of a G Major arpeggio. Each measure actually contains a different pattern but if you play the notes fluidly (using either technique mentioned above) and watch your time, the entire exercise will sound like one whole rhythm pattern, which can be repeated over and over again.

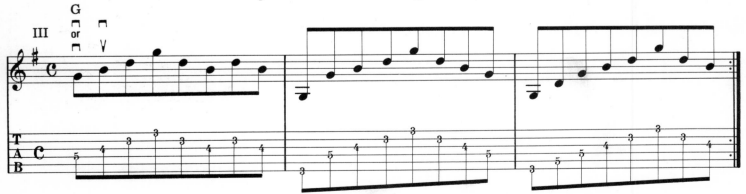

Now try this progression, played in arpeggiated style.

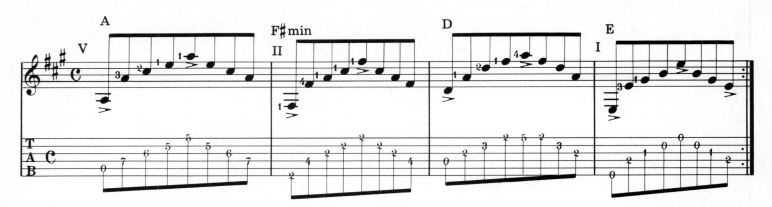

Arpeggios are often played with eighth-note triplets instead of regular eighth notes. A triplet is made up of three notes which receive the same number of beats or counts as two notes. In this case, since in $\frac{4}{4}$ time two eighth notes will receive one beat, an eighth-note triplet will also get one beat. Here's how eighth-note triplets look in musical notation.

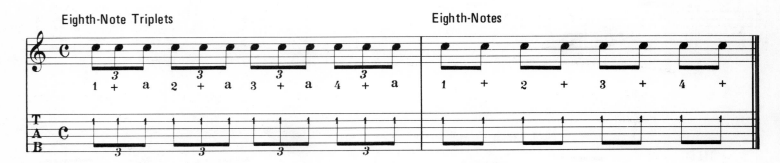

You can see that there are four eighth-note triplets (twelve notes altogether) in a measure, and that there is always a "3" written above the triplet, to help you identify it as such when it appears in a piece of music. You can also see that eighth-note triplets are counted "1 + a, 2 + a, 3 + a, 4 + a" instead of "1 + 2 + 3 + 4 + ." Here is a simple arpeggio played over the changes to a popular song, "End of the World." Remember, count " 1 + a, 2 + a, etc.," because you are now playing eighth-note triplets. Go slowly at first until your rhythm sounds steady and even, then increase your speed up to a moderate tempo.

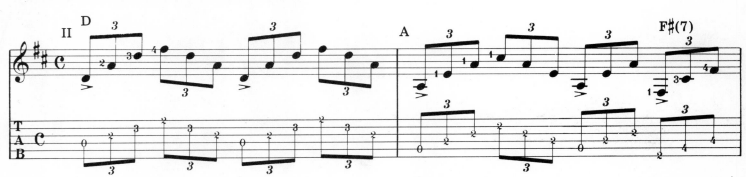

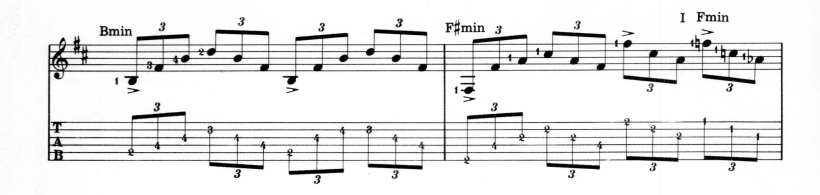

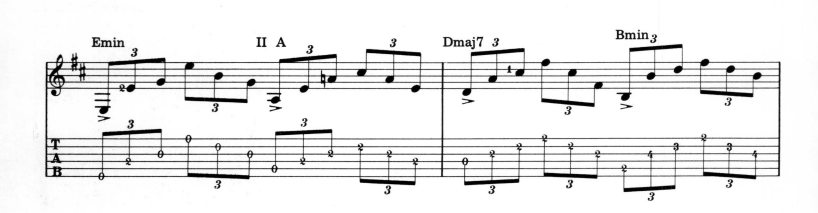

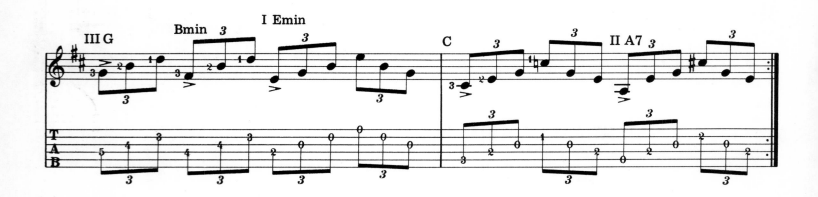

Muted Arpeggios

Another technique of playing arpeggios is to *mute* them. When a note is muted, it doesn't ring out and sustain; instead you get a deadened, "choked" sound. There are two ways of muting a note: one, using the left-hand fingers and two, using the fleshy part of the right-hand palm. For now, we will deal only with the technique of muting with the right hand.

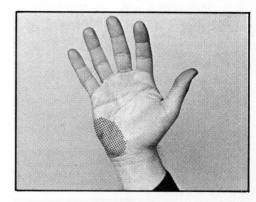

To mute a note, rest the fleshy part of the right-hand palm lightly upon the strings just before the bridge of the guitar (between the bridge and the soundhole on an acoustic or between the bridge and the pickup on an electric). The flesh of your right-hand palm will stop the string from vibrating shortly after the note has been picked. Study these pictures and then try playing some muted notes, varying the position and angle of your right-hand until you get the sound you like.

Here are two rhythm riffs using muted arpeggios. The first one uses eighth notes and the second uses eighth-note triplets. Getting all of the notes to sound equally muted or deadened should be your goal. If some notes sound more muted than others, you are probably not resting your palm evenly across all of the strings. After practicing these exercises, make up arpeggios of your own and play them with and without muting the notes. The symbol I will use throughout the rest of the book for muting a string with your right hand is "MR" written directly below the note.

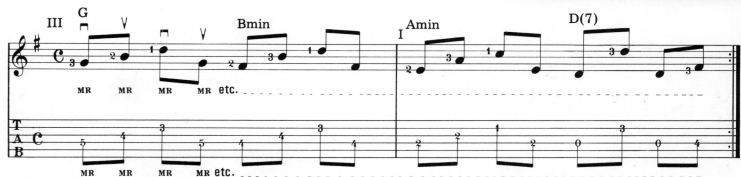

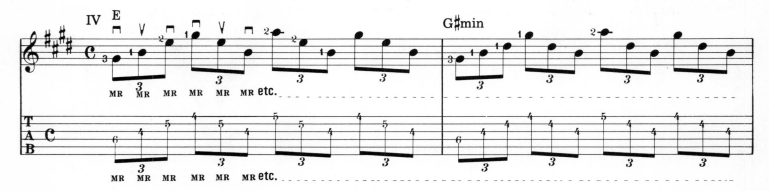

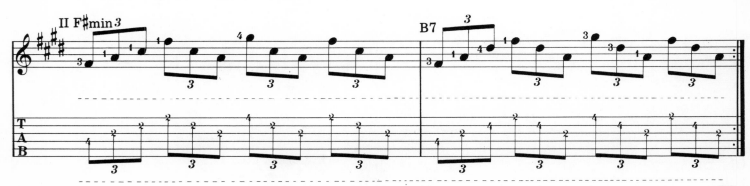

Muted Bass Riffs

You can use the muting technique described above to pick a variety of rhythm riffs on the bass strings. Artists such as Chuck Berry and Steve Miller often play these bass rhythms along with a chorded rhythm or alone, to create an interesting rhythm feel. Play these rhythms and try varying the degree to which you mute the notes, from slightly choked to very muted, by changing the amount of pressure you put on the strings with your right-hand palm.

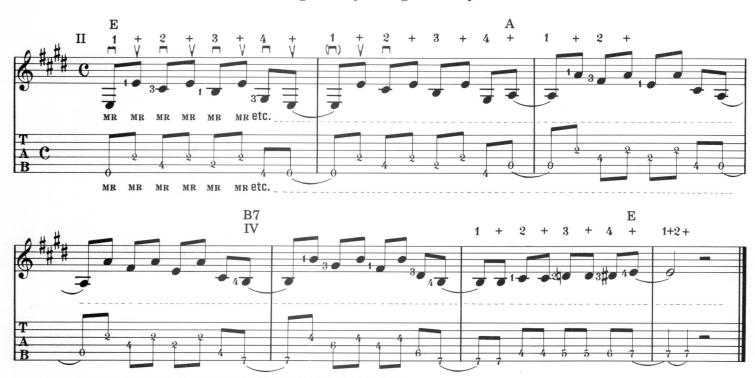

Notice that in the previous exercise, the chords do not change at the beginning of each measure. Instead, they change on the last eighth note of each measure—the "and" in between beats four and one of the next measure. This is quite common in rock songs and is known as anticipating the chord or changing on the upbeat. In the next rhythm, the chords change on beat one of every measure (as usual).

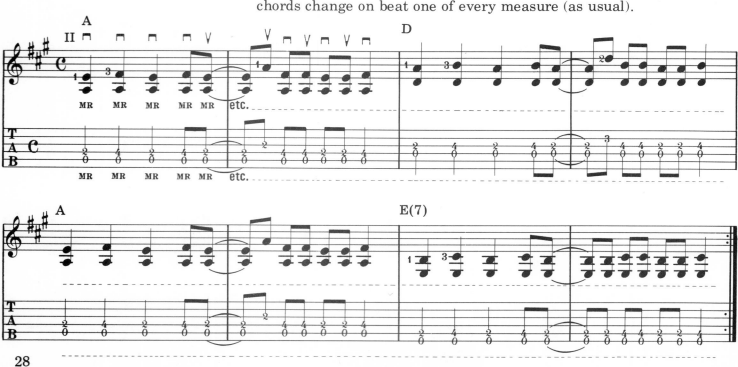

Rhythm Review

At this point I would like to suggest a review of what you've learned in the first part of the book. Before you reach the next few chapters, which cover very important and slightly more advanced rhythm concepts, you should be able to play (and play *in time*!) everything we've talked about so far. Here is a good way to review all of the material which has been presented.

1. Pick a chord progression from the first part of the book. Turn on your metronome and record the progression on a cassette tape recorder. Record the same progression a few times so you won't have to keep rewinding the tape in order to hear the rhythm over and over.
2. Play back what you've recorded and
   a. Play partial chords in various positions and inversions against the recorded rhythm.
   b. Play alternating bass rhythms along with the tape.
   c. Play arpeggios over the chords.
   d. Play muted arpeggios and muted bass riffs against what you've recorded.
   e. Play various rhythms along with the tape; see which ones sound good and which don't.

Then do the same thing with different progressions, either those I've written out or those which you've made up yourself. Practice and practice and soon, you will notice a difference in your playing; it will get better!

Rhythm Patterns

Dotted Eighth and Sixteenth Notes

The music in this chapter will be a little more advanced than that in the earlier part of the book. We will be playing dotted eighth notes and sixteenth notes. A dotted eighth-note looks like this:

A dot after a note increases its value or duration by one half. In this case, the G note would get one half a beat plus one quarter beat or three quarters of a beat (½ beat + ¼ beat = ¾ beat). A sixteenth note looks like this:

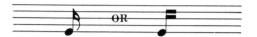

A measure made up entirely of sixteenth notes looks like this:

When counting sixteenth notes, count "1 a + a, 2 a + a, 3 a + a, 4 a + a" (sixteen counts). You now see that a dotted eighth note equals three sixteenth notes: 1/8 + 1/16 or 2/16 + 1/16 = 3/16. Therefore you would count a dotted eighth-note "1 a + ." Here is a sample measure including both dotted eighth notes (which can also be written as a tied eighth and sixteenth note) and sixteenth notes.

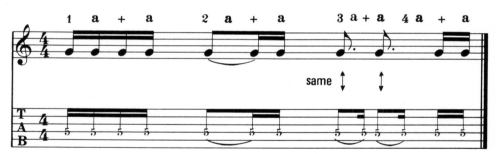

Here are some rhythm patterns which both sound good and will give you practice in reading. They are all written in the key of C Major; some of the progressions may sound familiar to you as they have been used in many popular rock songs.

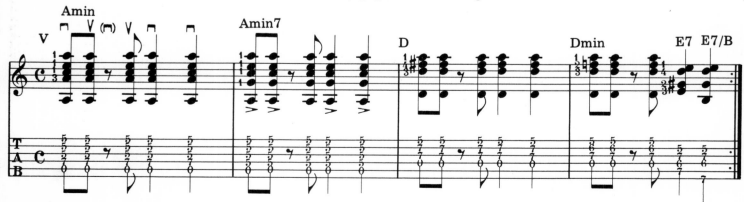

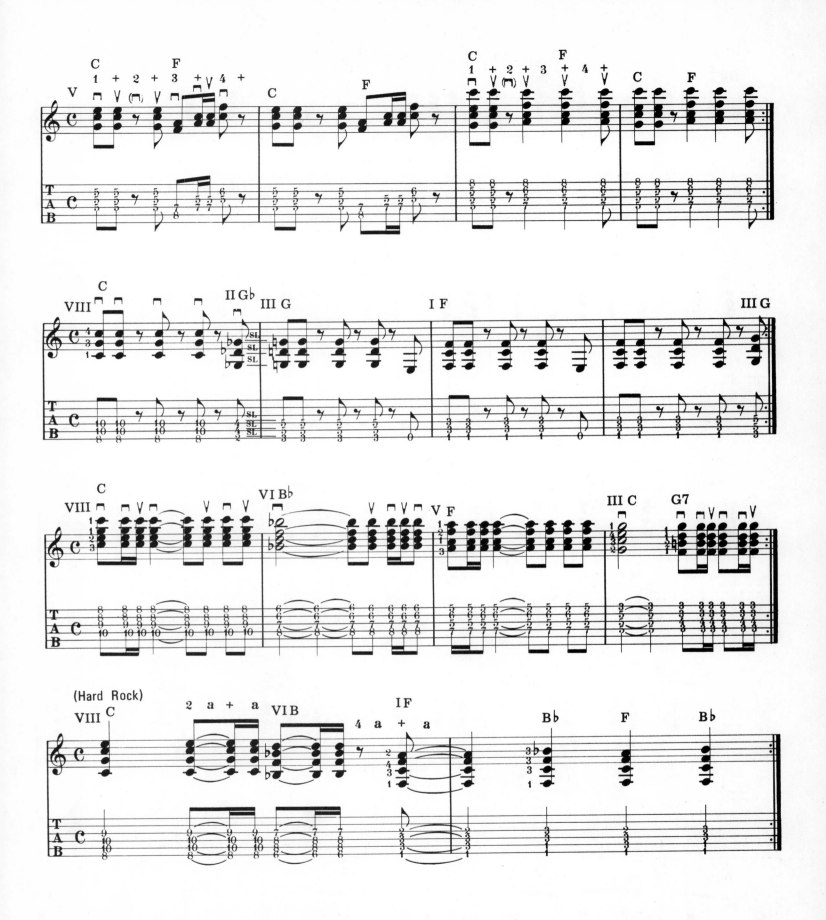

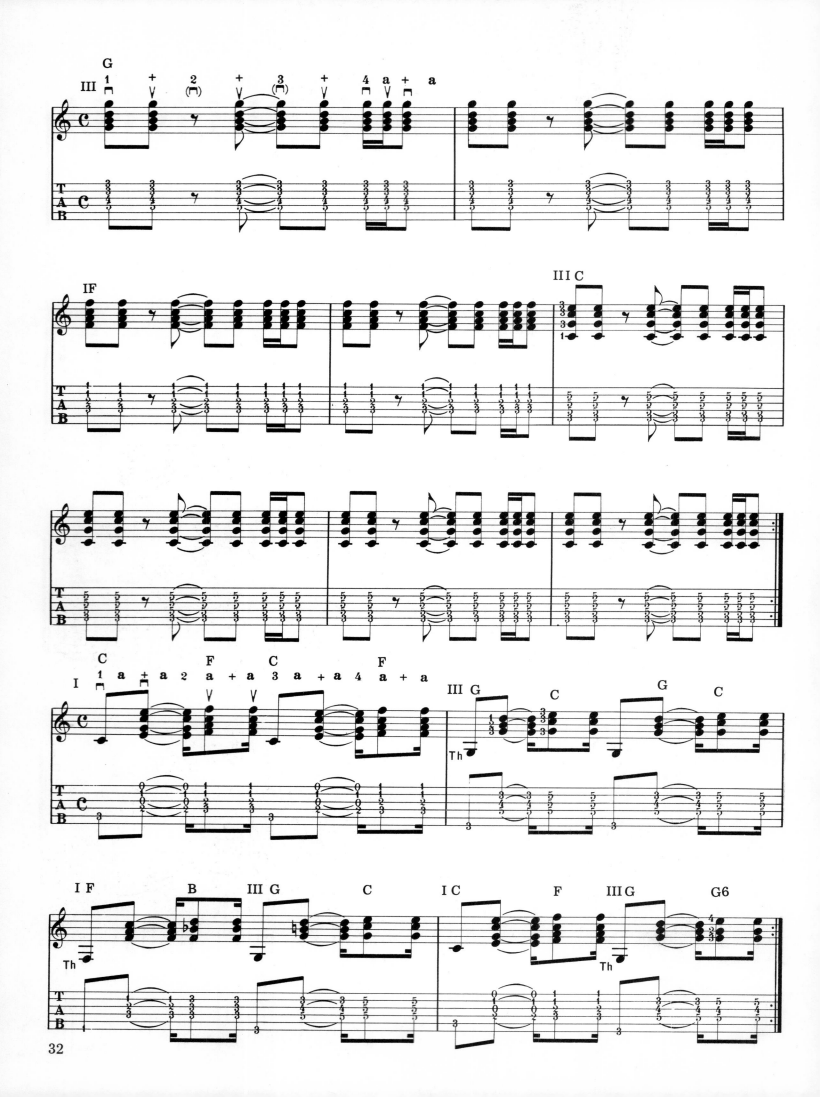

32

Slap-Damping

After having played over these rhythms a few times (remember, slowly at first), you might think that they sound a little choppy in the parts where you are resting and not playing. There is a technique for keeping the rhythm flowing throughout the rests and I call it "slap-damping." It is really muting the strings and strumming the muted strings. Here is how you do it.

1. Slightly lift your *left* hand off the notes you are fingering, so that your fingers are still on the strings but are not pressing them all the way down to the fingerboard.

2. Strum as usual with your *right* hand, but at the same time that you come down with your hand, mute the strings with the flesh of your right palm. This highly coordinated movement will take quite a bit of practice to really get down. Don't be discouraged. Once you accomplish this technique, your rhythm playing will sound as good as that of the finest guitarists around.

These photographs illustrate both the left and right-hand positions in slap-damping.

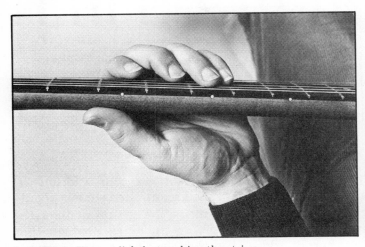

Left Hand: Fingers lightly touching the strings.

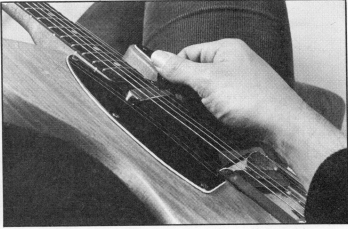

Right Hand: Just before you strum.

Right Hand: Upon contact with the strings.

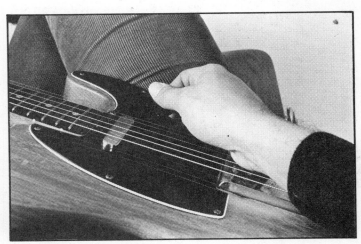

Right Hand: After strum.
Note: Right palm is still touching the strings.

Now try this technique, first with quarter-note rhythms, then with eighth-note patterns. It's a good idea to go back over the few rhythms I just gave you and play them with the slap-damping technique. But first, study these examples. I will use an "S" written below the staff to symbolize the slap-damping strum of a chord.

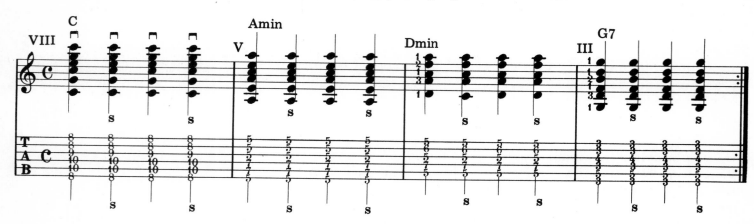

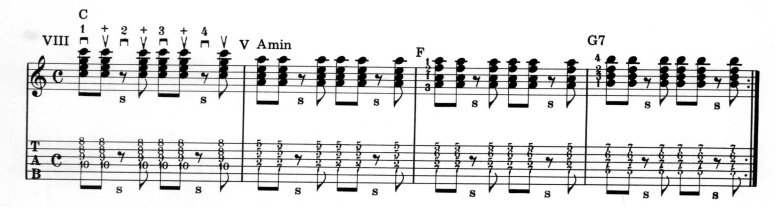

Notice that you are usually slap-damping on the second and fourth beats of each measure. This goes back to what I mentioned earlier about the primary accents in popular music coming on the second and fourth beats. By slapping the guitar, you are giving an extra push to the rhythm section and are thereby adding tightness and drive to the music. Accenting the second and fourth beats will also help your timing because it gives you an anchor into the playing of the drummer and bassist.

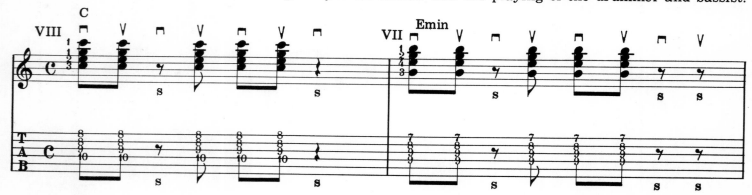

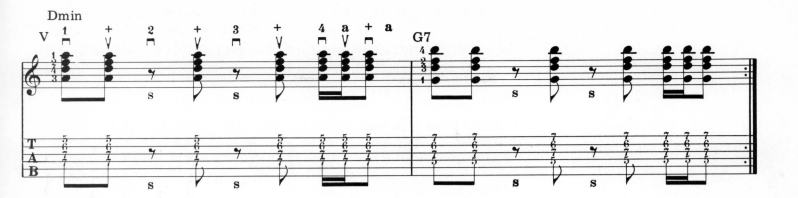

In the above example, you are slap-damping on an upbeat—the last beat of the E minor chord—as well as a downbeat. The technique of damping on an upbeat is basically the same as that which you learned for a downbeat, the difference being that you bring your right-hand palm down to mute the strings in the opposite direction.

Here's another rhythm for you to practice your slap-damping on. Remember, use up- and downstrokes and start off at a tempo slow enough to allow your time to be steady and even.

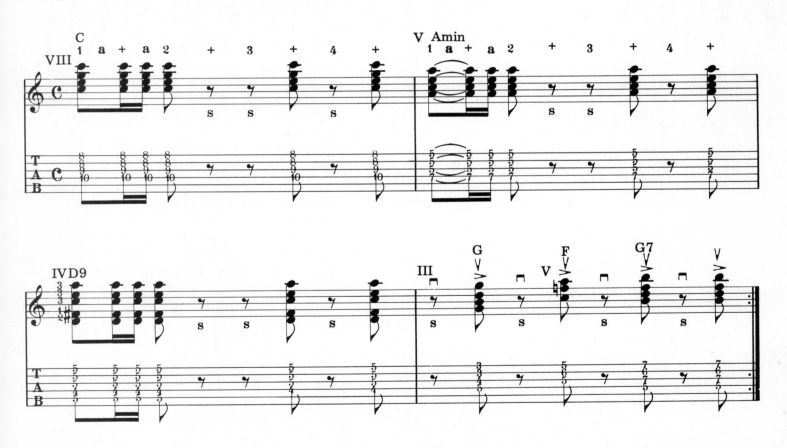

The Sixteenth Rest

This next rhythm introduces the sixteenth rest. It looks like this:

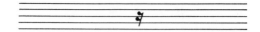

When a sixteenth rest appears in the music, rest for one sixteenth count or one quarter beat. This rest has the same duration as a sixteenth note, one quarter of a beat, when the music is written in $\frac{4}{4}$ or common time. Try these rhythms which incorporate sixteenth rests into what you have been doing.

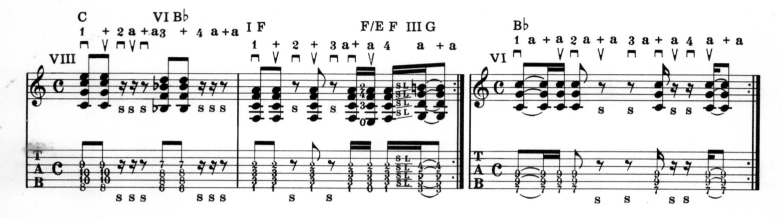

Transposing Chord Progressions

The rhythms I have just given you can be played in any key, not just in C Major. Changing music from one key to another is known as *transposition*. In order to transpose, you first have to know a little about music theory. The following few pages are very important for the complete understanding of the rest of the book. Read them slowly and try to relate what is said to what you know already about rhythm guitar.

The Major Scale

A major scale is a series of eight notes arranged in a pattern of whole steps and half steps. This is the series of notes known as the *C Major scale*.

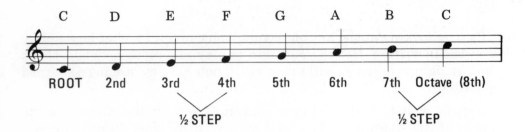

You see that between E and F and between B and C there is one half step. A whole step is equal to two frets on the guitar and a half step is equal to one fret. Except for E to F and B to C, there is a whole step between all the other notes. The distance from one note to another is called an *interval*. The intervals in the C Major scale are as follows:

Scale Tone	(Note)	Interval
Root	C	
2nd	D	Whole Step
3rd	E	Whole Step
4th	F	Half Step
5th	G	Whole Step
6th	A	Whole Step
7th	B	Whole Step
Octave—8th	C	Half Step

This interval pattern holds true for every major scale. With the above information you can construct any major scale! Start first with the name of the scale and therefore the first note in the scale. Then go up to the next interval (a whole step) and write down the name of the note there. Proceed in this manner, remembering that between the third and fourth and seventh and eighth there is a half step, until you reach the octave (eighth note). Here is an example of this technique, using the D Major scale.

Key Signature

In order to keep the same interval pattern of whole and half steps that we used in the C Major scale, the F and C notes have to be *sharped*, or raised one half step each, giving us an F♯ and C♯ in the D Major scale. Therefore, the *key signature* for D Major is "two sharps." When a piece of music is written in a particular key, as all music is, the key signature tells you which notes have to be either sharped (♯) or flatted (♭) in order to maintain the proper scale-interval relationship for the notes in that key. If we want to "cancel" a sharp or flat at any point in the music, a *natural* sign (♮) is used. For example, if we were playing in the key of D Major, this note

would be played as a C natural, not a C sharp. The natural sign applies only in the measure in which it is used. It must be notated again in later measures if we want to cancel another *accidental* (a sharp or a flat).

By first looking at the key signature, you can tell in what key a piece of music is written. Before you begin to play any piece of music, check the key signature so you will know which notes, if any, are to be sharped or flatted!

Here is a list of Major key signatures. You should memorize the names of the sharps and flats for each key, or at least for each key we have covered so far in this book.

Major Key Signatures

C		**No sharps or flats**
G		**One sharp** F♯
D		**Two sharps** F♯ -C♯
A		**Three sharps** F♯ -C♯ -G♯
E		**Four sharps** F♯ -C♯ -G♯ -D♯
B		**Five Sharps** F♯ -C♯ -G♯ -D♯ -A♯
F♯		**Six sharps** F♯ -C♯ -G♯ -D♯ -A♯ -E♯
F		**One flat** B♭
B♭		**Two flats** B♭-E♭
E♭		**Three flats** B♭-E♭-A♭
A♭		**Four flats** B♭-E♭-A♭-D♭
D♭		**Five flats** B♭-E♭-A♭-D♭-G♭
G♭		**Six flats** B♭-E♭-A♭-D♭-G♭-C♭

Diatonic Chords

Chords within a given key are called *diatonic chords*. Major and minor chords are composed of three notes, and the three-note chords are called *triads*. The numerical relationship between the notes of these triads is 1–3–5. For example, to build a C Major chord, we start on C (1), add the third note in the C Major scale, E, and then the fifth, G. Therefore the notes in a C Major chord are C, E and G.

If we now build chords starting on each note of the C Major scale, here is what we get:

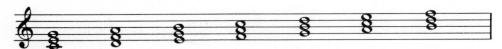

I-Cmajor . II-Dminor . III-Eminor . IV-Fmajor . V-Gmajor . VI-Aminor . VII-Bdiminished.

We need not be concerned with the B diminished chord now, as diminished chords are hardly used at all in rock music and therefore are not emphasized in this book.

If you construct triads containing only the notes of the scale upon any major scale, you will get the same pattern of chords. The pattern looks like this:

Major Scale Chords	I	II	III	IV	V	VI	VII
	Major	minor	minor	Major	Major	minor	diminished

Here is the importance of this formula: Knowing the notes of any major scale allows you to construct the basic chords in that key!

Try building the chords of some keys I have already used in this book, such as G, F, A, D and E. See what you come up with; play them; see if they sound "right" or "wrong." Remember, the II, III and VI chords are always *minor* and the I, IV and V chords are always *Major*, when you are working within major keys.

Chord Progression

As I mentioned earlier, some chords seem to "go together" more naturally than others. This section will help you to understand the reasons why this is so. The basic chord in any key is the "key chord" itself, called the *tonic* or the *I chord*. The next most important chord in a key is the chord which is built on the fifth step of the key; this V chord is called the *dominant* and usually leads back to the I chord (the tonic). This V-I progression is the basis for most music in the Western world. Very often the V chord has a fourth note added to it, this note being the fourth note in the major scale. For example, in the key of C Major, the V chord is a G; adding an F note to the G makes it a G^7 (the V^7 chord). The third most important chord in a key is called the *sub-dominant* or the IV chord. Together with the tonic and the dominant, the sub-dominant rounds out the three basic chords in any key. Thousands of songs have been written using only these three chords.

Transposing

Now that you know about scales and keys and diatonic chords, transposing becomes a very simple matter. Let's look at the following chord progression, in the key of G Major.

Notice that the progression begins on the I chord (G), goes to the III (minor), E minor, then to the II (minor), A minor. Then it goes to an F Major, which is *out of the key of G Major,* and then to the V⁷ chord (D⁷). If we want to transpose this progression to the key of E Major, the first chord would be an E (the I chord), then a C♯ minor (III), then an F♯ minor (II), then a D Major, and finally a B⁷ (the V⁷ chord). Since the relationship between the G and F chords in the original progression is *down a whole step,* we use this same relationship in finding that in the key of E Major, the chord corresponding to the F Major in the first progression is a D Major—one whole step down from E.

In general, when transposing from one key to another, find out what chord intervals are used in the original progression and then apply this formula to the new series of chords. If you are writing out the music, remember to notate the proper key signature.

Rolling Stone Ron Wood with Joe Walsh of the *Eagles*

Basic Chord Progressions

Now that you know how to transpose from one key to another, we will go over some basic progressions; once you have mastered these in the given key, you should transpose and play them in other keys.

I- IV- V⁷   Starts on the I chord of the key (the tonic), goes to the fourth and then to the fifth. For example, G-C-D⁷.

I- II- V⁷   Again, starts on the tonic, moves to the II chord (which is a minor chord) and then to the fifth. For example, A-Bmin-E⁷.

I-VI-II-V⁷   Tonic, sixth (minor), second (minor) and fifth, such as C-Amin-Dmin-G⁷.

You can see that the first and second progressions are almost the same. In general, you can substitute a II chord for a IV chord (and vice-versa) in most progressions. For example, E-A-B⁷ becomes E-F♯ min-B when an F♯ min chord is substituted for the A chord. Here are examples of these various progressions, and some more in addition. Remember, the Roman numerals above the staff refer to positions, not chords.

I-IV-V⁷

The quarter-note triplet at the end of this rhythm is played in two beats: three quarter notes written as a triplet, or two quarter notes.

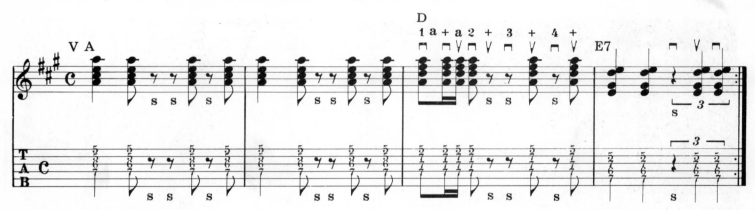

V⁷-IV-I

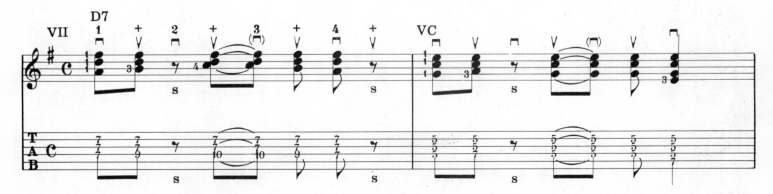

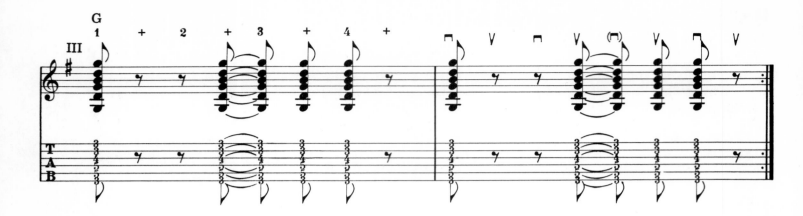

I-II-V⁷

The G¹³ chord is a substitution for G⁷.

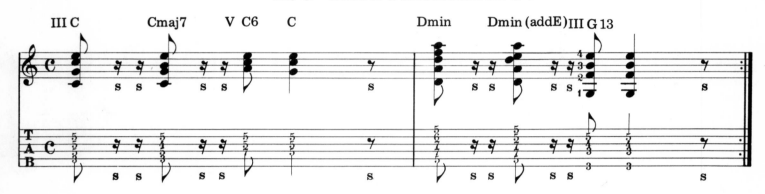

I-II-IV-V⁷

The B⁹ chord is a substitution for B⁷.

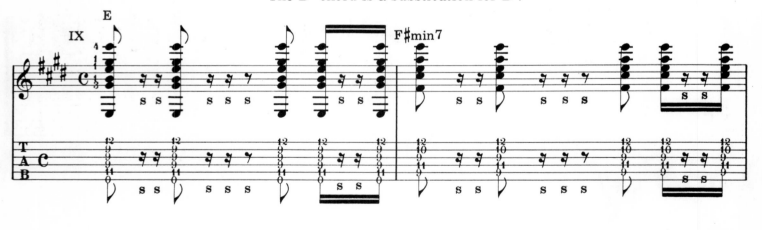

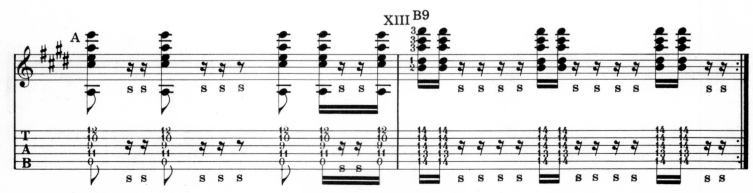

I-VI-II-V⁷

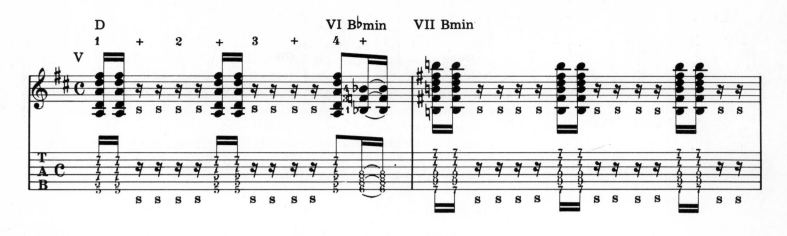

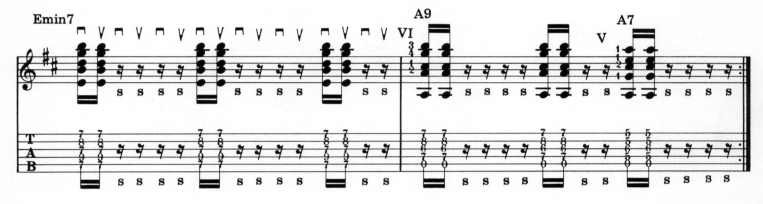

VI-IV-V

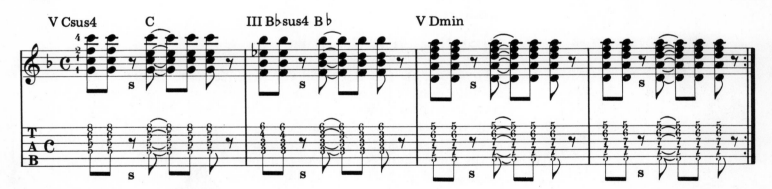

VI-II-V

The A minor ⁷ and D⁷ in the last measure of the rhythm are passing
chords to bring you from B♭ back to G minor.

Playing Rhythm Guitar

If you have really learned the material presented in the preceding pages, you now have enough technical knowledge, theoretical understanding and facility in playing rhythm styles to be able to play rhythm guitar with other musicians. But what if you get together with a drummer, bassist and horn player and they say, "OK, let's do "Get Back" (by the *Beatles*) in G?" What do you do? How do you begin? This chapter will focus on the practical aspects of *doing it* . . . playing rhythm guitar.

Some Points to Consider

When I play rhythm guitar, I try to make what I am playing

1. Interesting and pleasing to the ear, so it sounds good.
2. Relevant to the song, so it sounds right.
3. In touch with the other musicians' playing, so we sound together.
4. Steady and even with respect to the time of the music, so everything sounds tight.

You may be wondering, "What is an 'interesting' rhythm?", or "How can I play 'in touch' with the other players?" Well, there are quite a few musical variables which can be altered to accomplish these ends. You can play either full or partial chords in various positions and inversions, use upstrokes or downstrokes and combinations of both, play louder or softer, vary your tone from bass to treble (and vary your tone within a song), play in a fluid or choppy style, use various rhythm techniques (like playing arpeggios or muted bass riffs), use substitution chords, and play eighth-note, sixteenth-note or triplet patterns. It is your job as a rhythm guitarist to call upon all of your knowledge and *experiment* in order to create the rhythm which sounds best for a particular tune.

Creating the Rhythm

Let's look at "Get Back", in G Major. You, the bassist and drummer are all ready to go, plugged in, tuned up, and the drummer counts off "1–2–3–4." Right away you know the *tempo* (speed) the song will be played at, the time signature ($\frac{4}{4}$ or common time), and you know the key (G Major). At this point I will assume that you know the changes to the song. Since "Get Back" is a rock song on the "hard" side, try to get a powerful rhythm sound (see the earlier chapter on Power Chords). First try a quarter-note pattern; this one is a rhythm riff built around the basic changes to the song, G-C-G.

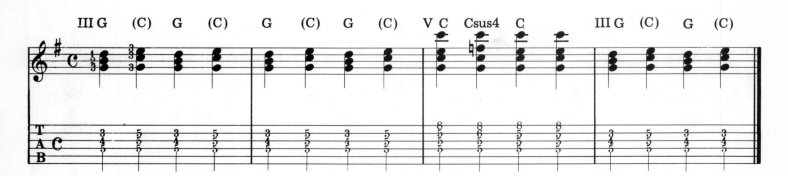

Well, it sounds OK but not really *right*; therefore your group probably won't sound together—like a band—if you play this rhythm. There is nothing actually bad about this rhythm; the idea or germ for an interesting rhythm is there, but it doesn't quite make it yet—it needs work. What's missing? What's wrong? First, you might notice that this rhythm has no "bottom" to it. Let's try something in a lower octave, on the bass strings.

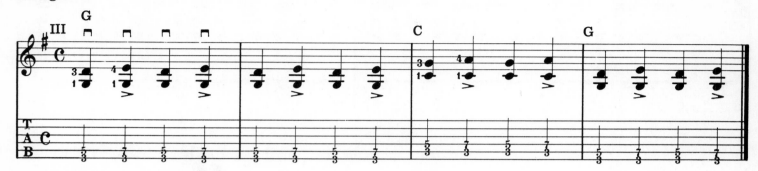

What a difference! Now we've got the basic sound down. But there doesn't seem to be any energy or drive or life to the rhythm. Let's double up on the rhythm, using eighth notes instead of quarter notes, and see how that sounds.

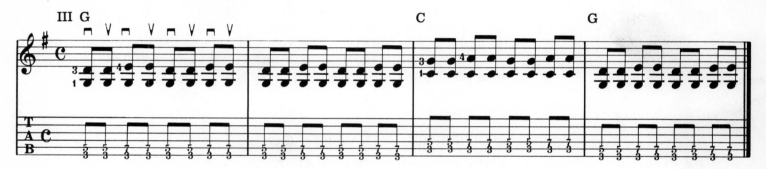

Look at how much progress has been made by just changing two variables: the tonality of the chord and the rhythm pattern. Now let's change two more: use only downstrokes instead of alternating picking and slap-damp the second and fourth beats of each measure. Also, play the C chord in the eighth position (it's easier to downstroke it there).

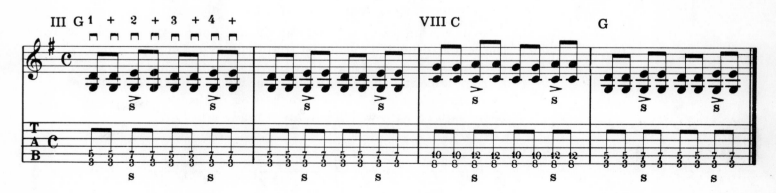

Now this sounds really great! And if your drummer happens to be playing a "rolling" rhythm, as Ringo Starr does on the record, this next rhythm pattern will complement his playing. Then you can alternate between this rhythm and the previous one to further vary your sound.

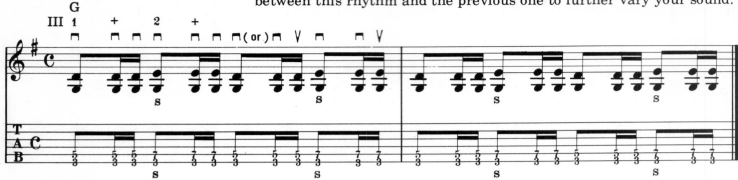

Once again, playing great rhythm guitar is not magic! You can see that by *systematic experimentation* you can create interesting, solid rhythms.

Now obviously I can't take you through the changes and rhythms to every rock song you might encounter. What you have learned from the preceding example ("Get Back") is that getting the "right" rhythm for a song has a lot to do with experimentation. The more you play, and play with others, the more valuable experience you will gain. The more experience you have, the less you will have to experiment in order to get a good rhythm part; you will intuitively know what will sound good and what won't.

Jamming: Varying Your Rhythm Playing Within a Progression

Sometimes you will get together with other musicians and instead of playing a complete song, you will just "jam" over a series of changes. This kind of playing is lots of fun and can be very instructive, since you can pick up rhythms and riffs from the other players from listening to what they are doing. On the other hand, some jams can get very boring if everyone keeps playing the same thing over and over again.

As a rhythm guitarist, you can change your playing subtly to vary the sound even if the bassist and drummer are repetitious in their playing. Of course, if the other players change what they are playing to complement your variations, you will be free to experiment even more. Let's look at a I-IV-V^7 progression in the key of G major—a very basic pattern with which you are already familiar.

If you were jamming on the above progression, your first rhythm might be a medium-rock feel based on a syncopated eighth-note pattern, as follows.

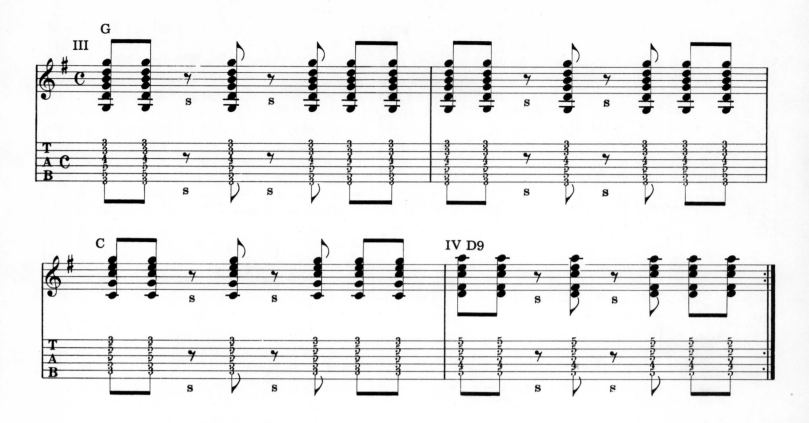

Now look at the first variation below. Play it.

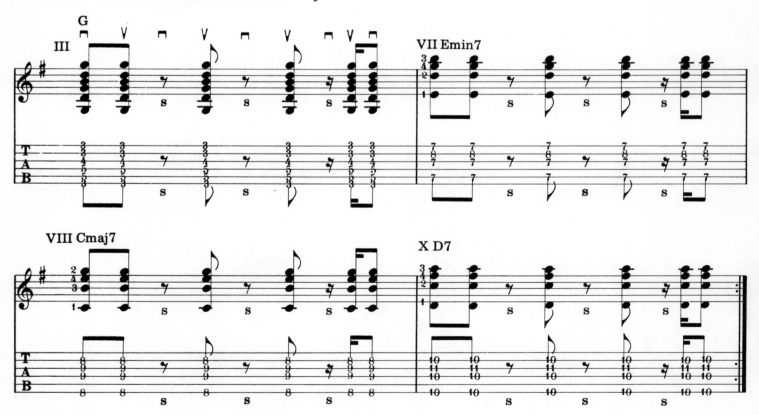

You have varied your rhythm pattern slightly (notice the use of sixteenth notes on the last beat of measures 1 and 2) but still managed to keep the same feel. Also, an E^{min7} has been substituted for a G chord in the second measure as well as a C^{maj7} for a C and a D^7 for the D^9. In the following example, the further variations include playing a bass riff against the changes, using partial chords in various positions and switching from up and downstrokes to only downstrokes in the last two measures.

The next variation is really just a 4 measure bass riff but I am introducing left hand muting in it. This technique is symbolized by an ML written directly under the note to be muted. To mute a string with your left hand, don't press the string all the way down to the fingerboard. Let your finger rest on the string to be muted and press down *slightly*, just enough so that you get some tone. If you don't press down on the string at all, the sound will be too dead and you won't be able to hear the pitch of the note. Practice this variation slowly at first until you get the muting technique down and then increase your speed.

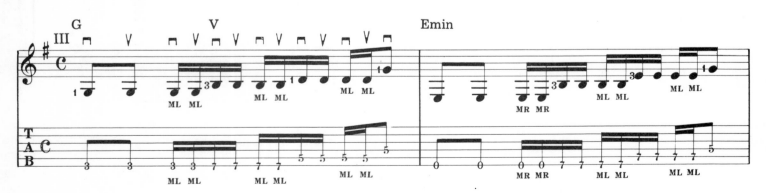

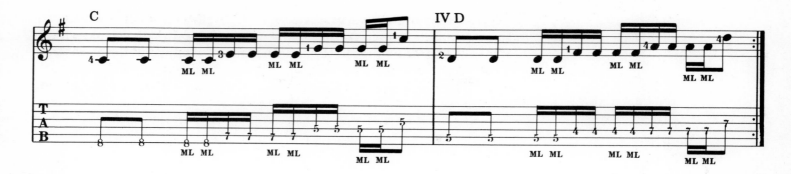

Let's get back to playing chords. Here's a funky rhythm over the same changes (G-C-D⁹). Try using your own inversions; vary the rhythms by yourself but remember to keep your playing steady and even.

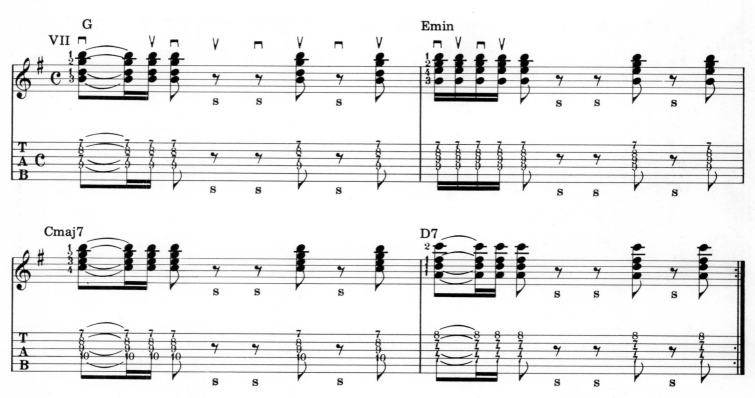

Here's a chordal riff using 3 different rhythm patterns. **Measures 1 and 3 use an even eighth note pattern played with downstrokes only. Measure 2 uses a funky rhythm and measure 4 combines a funky rhythm (on the A^{min}) with a sixteenth note triplet pattern (on the D^7). A sixteenth note triplet = 2 sixteenth notes or 1 eighth note in duration. Again, practice slowly at first and watch your time.**

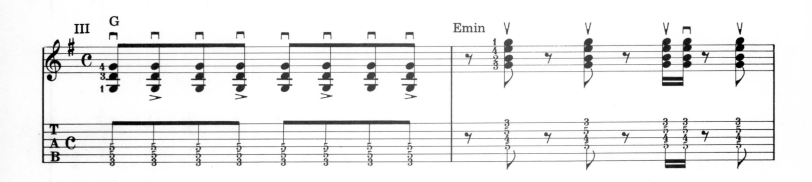

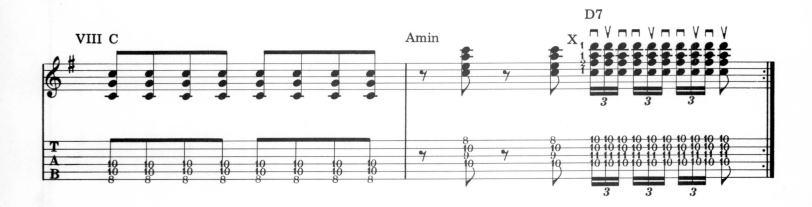

The last example in this section is a very melodic rhythm. **You are really playing a melody within the chords. This is done by using various substitution chords and inversions. The rhythm itself is quite simple but it may take you some practice to be able to change from one chord to the next without breaking time, so don't let those eighth notes fool you. This is a difficult rhythm pattern. Notice the following substitutions.**

G—G^{maj7}—G^{maj6}
E^{min}—E^{min7}—E^{min9}
A^{min}—A^{min7}—A^{min9}—F^{maj7}
D^7—$A^{min7}(C^{maj6})$—D^{7+5}

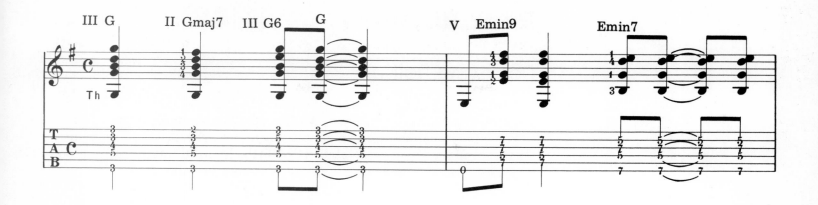

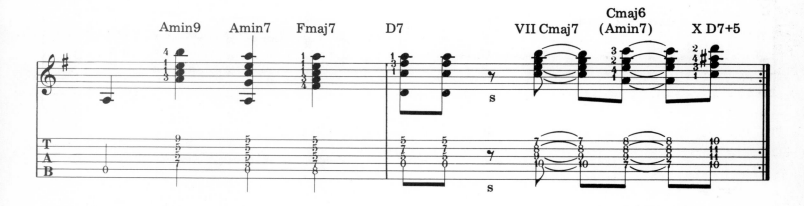

When jamming, you can also modulate from one key to another, using the same progression. Refer to the chapter on Transposing if you don't remember how to go from one key to another.

In the next chapter I will give you some ideas for rhythm patterns you can play for various kinds of tunes. Five categories will be covered: Rock and Roll, Hard Rock, Light Rock—Rock Ballad, Rhythm and Blues-Funk, and Disco. These categories are by no means mutually exclusive. For example, you might go to a "disco" feel in the bridge or middle of a rocker to lend variety to your rhythm sound. You should try mixing up the following rhythm patterns, remembering that your ear is the final judge of which rhythm makes it and which does not.

Rock Rhythms

Rock and Roll

Think of songs by artists such as Elvis Presley, Chuck Berry, the *Beatles*, the *Beach Boys*, Steve Miller, etc. The essence of these kinds of rhythms is a chugging, almost bouncy feel. Early Rock and Roll, such as the kind of music associated with Little Richard and Fats Domino, was not as syncopated (accented) as is today's popular music.

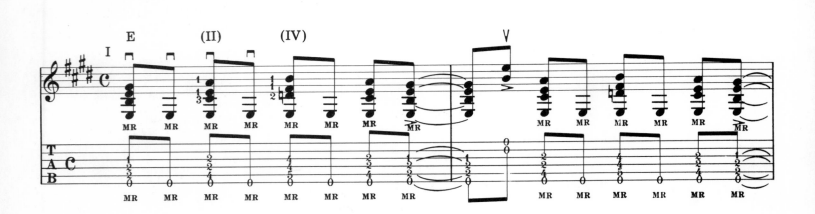

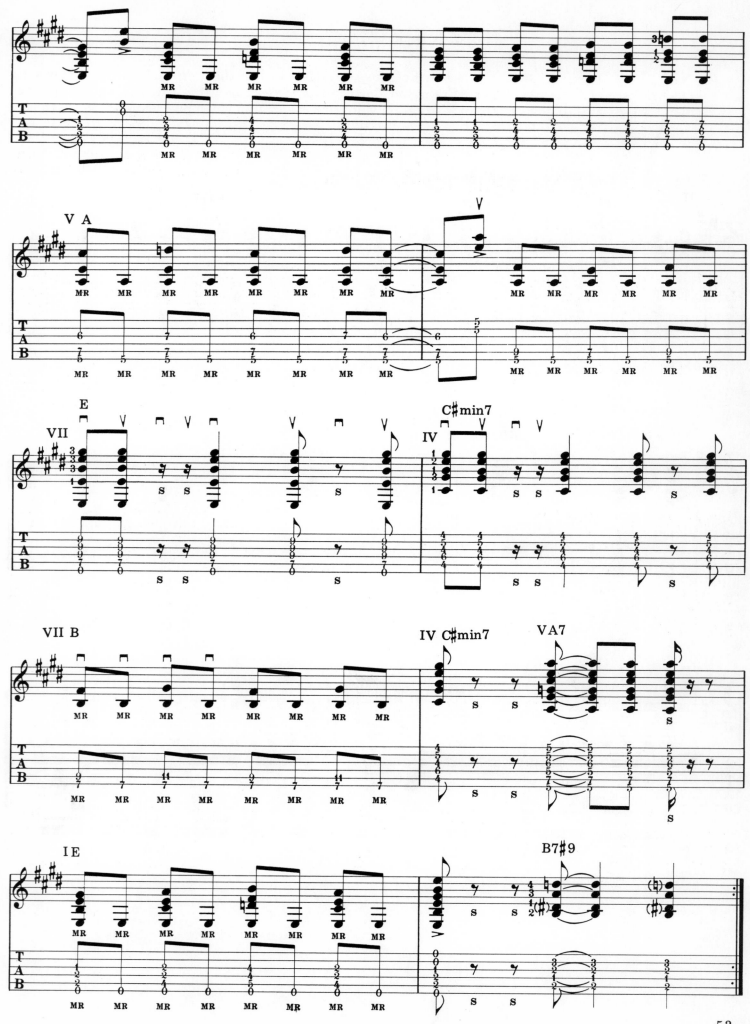

Hard Rock

Now think of songs by artists such as the *Rolling Stones*, Rod Stewart, Peter Frampton, *Bad Company, Fleetwood Mac*, the *Who*, etc. Use power chord settings on your guitar and amp when practicing these rhythms.

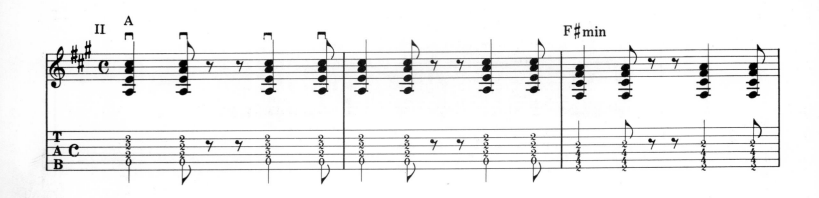

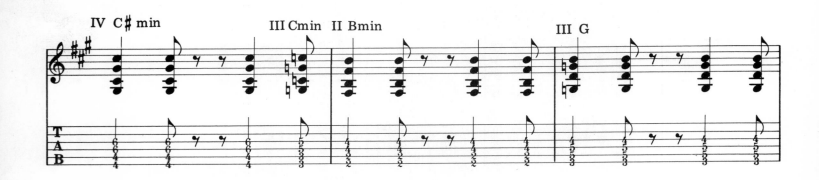

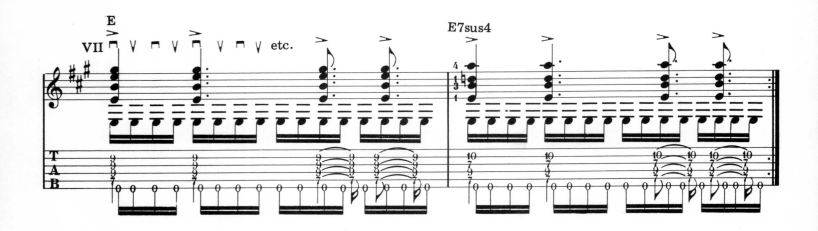

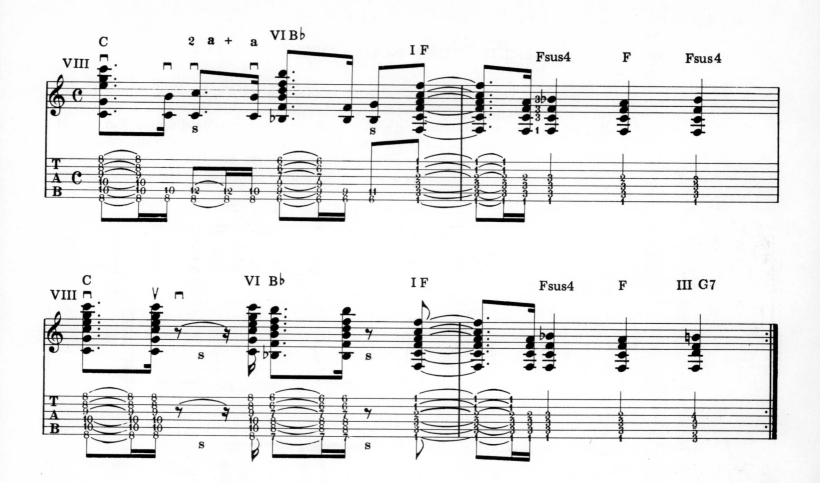

Light Rock—Rock Ballad

The characteristic rhythm in songs by the *Eagles*, Paul Simon, Carole King, Linda Ronstadt and others is an eighth-note feel, usually with the second and fourth beats of every measure slap-damped. Tunes with heavier country influence in this large pop field usually incorporate an alternating bass rhythm. These rhythms are fairly simple but very solid. Try copying the rhythm guitar parts off of the record to some popular songs.

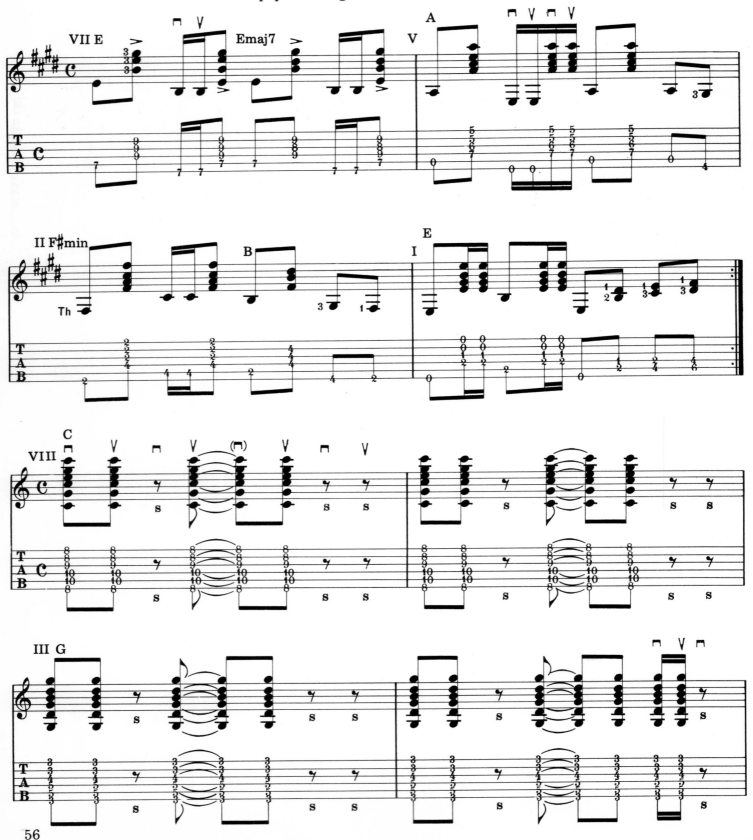

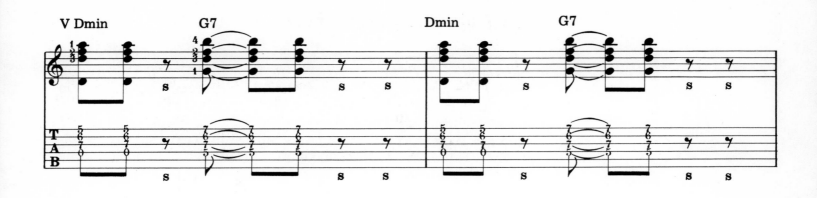

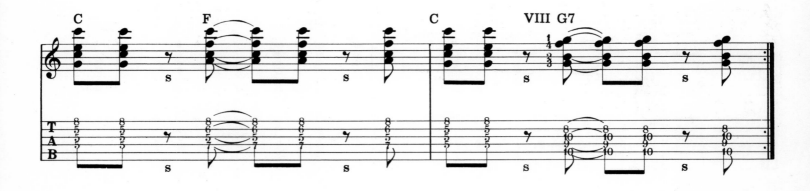

Rhythm and Blues—Funk

Songs by *Sam and Dave*, Otis Redding, *Booker T. and the MG's*, *Stuff*, the *Isley Brothers*, Marvin Gaye, *Earth, Wind and Fire*, and the *Average White Band* provide good illustrations of this next category. The rhythms for R & B material are usually highly syncopated mixtures of eighth and sixteenth notes. The first one here combines a few different rhythm patterns. A lot of "funk" rhythms are built around riffs, as in the second example below. Try making up your own rhythm riffs to popular songs you already know.

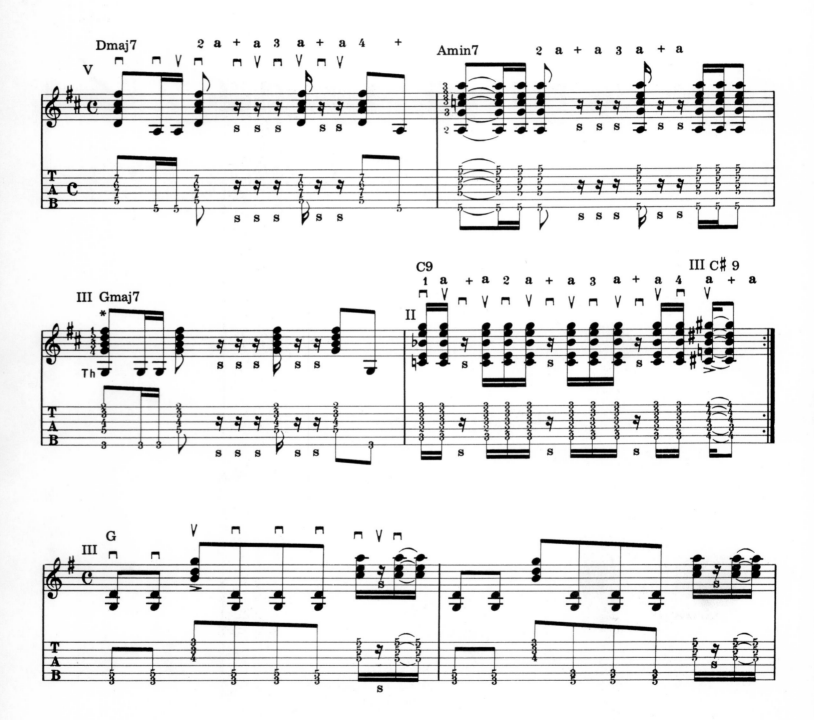

*Mute the A string with your thumb when playing this version of G Major 7.

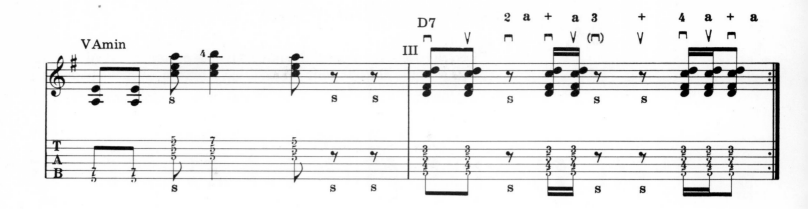

Jimi Hendrix

Disco

Disco rhythms are almost all sixteenth note patterns played in a very repetitive style. Here is your "basic disco" rhythm, as made popular by a very big recording star.

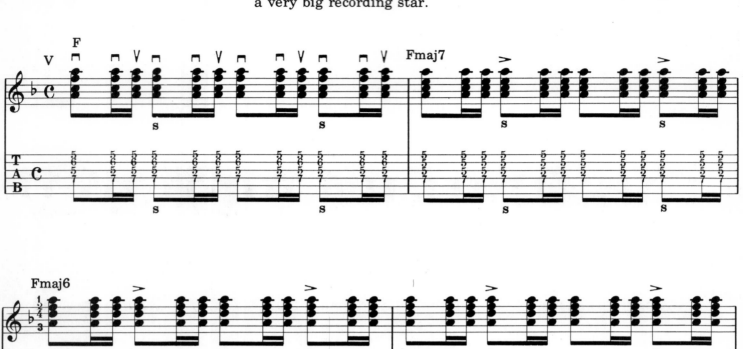

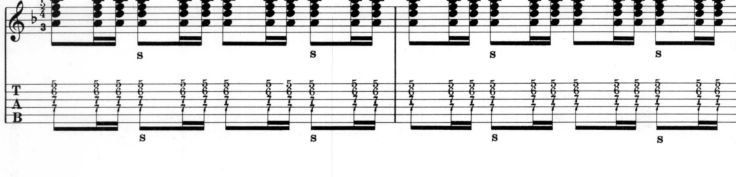

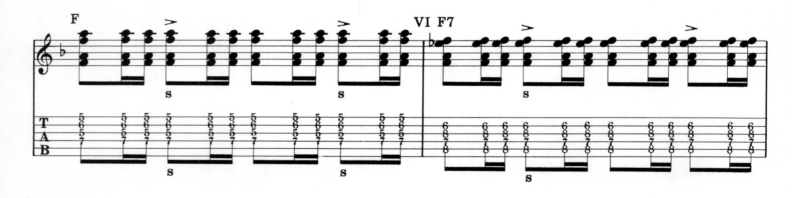

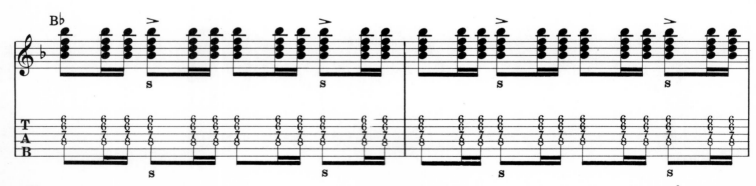

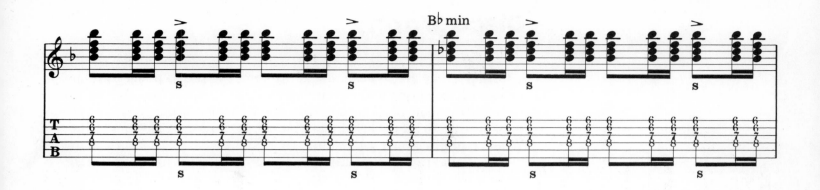

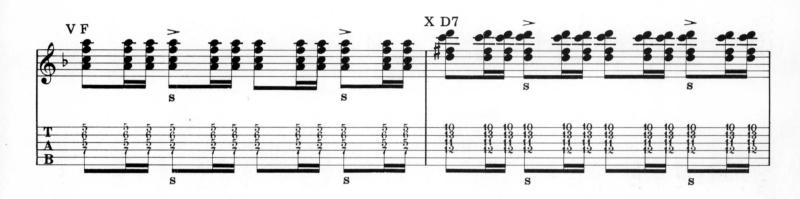

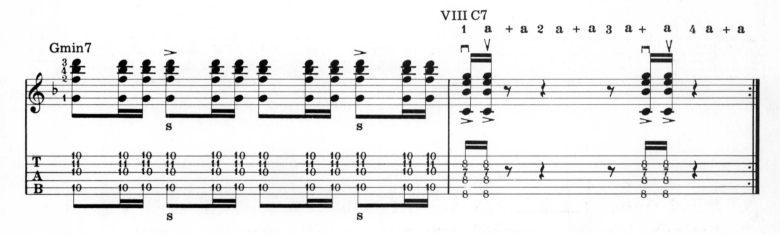

Discography

Rather than give you a list of specific records, I'll mention a few artists whose playing you should get to know. I'd like you to familiarize yourself with lots of different rhythm styles and sounds in order to open up your ears to all of the things that can be done by a rhythm guitarist. When listening to a particular song, try to hear the chord changes (without playing along). Listen to how the rhythm section creates a certain feel and note what accents and inversions the rhythm guitarist is playing to complement the melody of the song.

John Lennon
The greatest rhythm guitarist in modern rock music. A master of tone, time and taste. Listen to any (every) *Beatles* record.

George Harrison
What he does with partial chords—accents, bass riffs, arpeggios—is second only to his own leads with the *Beatles*.

Brian Jones and Keith Richard
Listen to their interplay and contrasting sounds on many early *Rolling Stones* records. My favorite albums are *Out of Our Heads* and *Between the Buttons*.

Chuck Berry
Basic Rock and Roll rhythms. An early master of the art form. Check out his *Greatest Hits* album.

Jerry Reed
Listen to his rhythm style. Reed's syncopations against what are really just simple country-blues chord progressions are amazing.

Peter Townshend, Jeff Beck, Jimi Hendrix
The power chord players to listen to. Especially listen to Townshend on early *Who* cuts such as "I Can See For Miles," "Pictures of Lily," "Call Me Lightning," and others. My favorite Hendrix album is *Axis: Bold As Love* and ditto for Beck's *Truth*.

Rod Stewart's
solo albums (*Gasoline Alley, Every Picture Tells A Story, Never A Dull Moment, A Night on the Town,*, etc.) feature many fabulous rhythm guitar players, from country-acoustic (Martin Quittenton) to hard rock (Ron Wood).

Steve Cropper and Cornell Dupree
practically invented R & B rhythm guitar. Listen to Cropper with *Booker T. and the MG's* and as a sideman with Otis Redding, among others; hear Cornell Dupree with his own N. Y. band, *Stuff*, as well as on many Aretha Franklin cuts. Both players define taste in rhythm playing.

Also check out: *Earth, Wind and Fire, Average White Band*, early Stax-Volt recordings on Atlantic (*Sam and Dave*, Otis, etc.), early Motown such as the *Supremes*, Stevie Wonder, Marvin Gaye (from the 1960s) and some rather good current artists, such as Peter Frampton, Steve Miller, and *Fleetwood Mac*.

Practice, play, listen, practice some more, keep good time, have a good time, and Good Luck!

Rolling Stones Mick Taylor, Mick Jagger and Keith Richard

New Books for the Rock Band

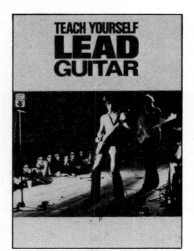

Teach Yourself Lead Guitar/EFS 200
by Steve Tarshis

Designed for the guitarist with some experience who wants to play exciting, professional-sounding lead guitar. This book teaches techniques, fingerings, riffs, blues scales, soloing and more. The music is all in standard notation and tablature, and a discography is included.

020200/$3.95

Teach Yourself Rock Bass/EFS 202
by David Gross

This book offers clear instruction for bass players who already have some familiarity with the instrument. A professional rock bassist teaches rock rhythms, blues progressions, scales, riffs, melodic patterns, all you need to know about buying equipment and more. The music is in standard notation and tablature, and a discography is included.

020202/$3.95

About the Author

Mark Michaels has studied guitar over a fifteen year period with such noted musicians as Carmine D'Amico and John Abercrombie. He divides his time between clubwork, recording, songwriting, concerts and teaching. At present, he is also guitarist for the New York City based band Fast Food. Mark is the author of three other Amsco publications: *Rock Riffs for Guitar, Rock Picture Chords,* and *Blues Riffs for Guitar.*